Shall WE Lead?

Leadership as a Partnership

Gage E. Paine, Ph. D.

For the early mentors and leaders who taught me how to lead and follow – Walter J. Urban, Sharon Justice, and Jim Caswell

Table of Contents

Introduction

"Dance and sing to your music. Embrace your blessings. Make today worth remembering."

Steve Marshall

The music starts, a mid-tempo bluesy song that makes me want to move. The instructor serving as tonight's DJ calls over the music, "Okay, everyone. This is a West Coast Swing. Find a partner and get out on the floor." Too bad. I only know the most basic steps – and not that well.

A senior dance instructor materializes in front of me with a beckoning hand. "Would you like to dance?"

I shake my head in regret. "I don't know much West Coast Swing."

Charming, he urges, "You'll know more when we're done."

Wondering just how much I am going to embarrass myself, I take his hand and follow him onto the dance floor.

He is right, of course. Because he is both an incredible dancer and a confident and capable leader, and because I have the necessary basic skills and am willing to follow, we dance a very fun West Coast Swing. It's not a mistake-free dance since I misread more than one lead, but we do a lot more than repeat the one basic step I know over and over.

The instructor kept his promise. By the end of the dance, I know a lot more about West Coast Swing than I had three minutes prior. I also know more about leading and following.

It takes a talented leader to help a novice partner achieve unexpected heights. Although this leader helped me dance above my level, he was limited by my skills and knowledge. We did a respectable dance, but if he had had a more advanced partner, he would have been able to lead more intricate patterns. He would have had more freedom to be creative.

Dance Isn't Just a Metaphor

I love to dance and I enjoy watching people dance. Ballroom, country and western, salsa – I love it all. I've always loved to dance, so much so that I began dancing to shows playing on television as soon as I could walk. I met my husband while taking dance lessons at Arthur Murray. Hokey, but true. I took ballroom dance lessons for six or seven years. Social dances, performances, competitions, I danced any way someone let me. As is always true of a complex, fascinating topic, the more I learned, the more I realized how much there was to learn.

When I discovered the world of ballroom dance, I had been teaching undergraduate leadership courses for several years. Trying to move students beyond books and theory was always a challenge, so I began to explore the idea of teaching leadership in new ways beyond the conventional, academic methods.

I played with novel approaches to understanding leadership, implementing varied and experimental methods to impress upon learners the importance of leadership as a practice. From this, the 12-week no-credit course Creative Leadership Workshop was born and subsequently offered to students and staff alike. Later, I created six-hour versions of the workshop, presenting it often as a part of the staff development classes offered through the Human Resources department on campus. From those intense workshops, I synthesized shorter segments for conference sessions.

The Leadership Dance is one of those abbreviated segments. It pulls together what I know about leadership and what I have learned about dance. Given its applicability and versatility, it is my most popular workshop, garnering groups as small as 20 and as large as 200! The Leadership Dance isn't just a useful metaphor; it really is about leading and following.

No matter the group size, it's always fun to lead this workshop since much of it is improvised. I never know exactly how the dance will unfold. There are steps and lessons that I include in every session, but the skill level and insight participants bring greatly influence the direction and progress of the program.

With its inherently kinesthetic lessons, the program is a dynamic reminder that dance and leadership are similar in that the only way to really learn either one is to get up and do it. And like ballroom dancing, leadership is best understood as a partnership, an equal partnership wherein participants have individual roles and responsibilities.

After facilitating countless iterations of The Leadership Dance, I have distilled, synthesized, and prioritized the workshops' essential material. So, here they are – lessons from The Leadership Dance.

Lesson 1

Leadership as a Partnership

"Music is the great unifier. An incredible force. Something that people who differ on everything and anything else can have in common."

Sarah Dessen

There's always someone who doesn't really believe it, someone who is sure that the title is just a metaphor and who blurts out in horror, "Wait, we're really going to dance?"

"Yes, we are. We're going to dance. Everyone stand up and form two concentric circles, inside-circle facing out, outside-circle facing in."

I can't blame them for being surprised, especially since many of my sessions are in professional settings. In fact, most seminar formats seem unconducive for such kinesthetic activities, providing only a few acceptable models for presentations (e.g. sitting in rows listening to a lecture, speeding through a few questions, and suffering through pair-and-share conversations). Even something as simple as sitting in a circle is unusual; getting up to move around is most certainly unexpected. And dancing? Nearly unimaginable. My workshop is so outside the norm, one participant actually walked out of a session. But, as is usually the case, everyone else shrugs and circles up.

Now, to introduce the dance. The participants in the inside circle are asked to start on their left foot while those in the outer circle facing them are tasked with beginning on their right, which sets them up to move in the same direction. I teach them the basic pattern of the Merengue (mer-en-gay), a simple, fun dance that only requires dancers to step on the beat – right, left, right, left. I follow that up by teaching a simple pattern: four steps to the left, four to the right, four steps backward, and four forward, thus expanding and contracting both circles.

There are a few missteps, a fair amount of chaos, and a great deal of laughter, but every group eventually succeeds, spontaneously breaking into applause when they come to a stop.

Pleased with their newfound confidence, I then explain dance convention – leaders start with the left foot, followers on the right. Abruptly, one group realizes they have been appointed leaders and are now responsible for the success of their pairings. Most of them are sure they aren't ready for the challenge.

I start the music. When "Suavemente" by Elvis Crespo rings out, smiles appear. After a few introductory claps to help them hear the beat, I count them in and the dance begins. Some stumble, others hesitate but are ushered forward by their more confident colleagues. The novice dancers complete several rounds using the new techniques I've taught them. Thereafter, I pause them and ask the followers to move one leader to the left. I restart the music and the dance begins again.

After dancing with two more partners, I stop the group and we talk. Leaders share their experiences dancing with different followers; followers speak about working with various leaders. Everyone talks about the ways the dance applies to working with individuals, groups, committees, and organizations.

Once the group has explored the edges of the metaphor, with a grin I ask them to switch roles – leaders become followers and followers become leaders for three additional rounds. Here, there are a lot of groans. Not only will they have to change roles, but now they must start on different feet.

After six rounds of dancing as well as learning how to perform and lead a basic underarm turn, it is clear to everyone that leaders and followers each have a responsibility to the success of the dance. The dance metaphor aptly illustrates leading and following as being equally important but different roles necessary for any partnership to flourish.

An Unconventional Learning Style

Although I have countless anecdotes to share regarding the success of this simple but effective exercise, there are a few that stand out to me. In one instance, a professor, who had been quite skeptical at the start of the workshop, approached me after a conference session. Unlike my colleague who had slipped out the door earlier, this participant stayed through the end. He had good things to say about the use of the metaphor as a way to teach and admitted he was glad to have stayed.

A year later at the same conference, I ran into him while looking for odds and ends at a convenience store. I recognized him and immediately said a pleasant hello.

"I remember you," he said, pointing at me. "You did the leadership dancing workshop-thing last year." He went on to list two or three memories from the workshop. "It was so difficult to dance with my partners in those first rounds when neither of us knew what we were doing. On the other hand, when I was dancing with followers who knew what they were doing, we did much better even when I was still learning the steps. I thought the whole workshop was a crazy idea at first, but I really get it now. The movement helps reinforce the lessons."

Learning through physical movement, otherwise known as kinesthetic learning, is a powerful tool, even for those who don't prefer it. In this case, it not only reinforced the specific lessons of the seminar, but poetically illustrated a dynamic point – people who want to lead or follow have to actually lead and follow. Reading about it simply isn't enough.

Kinesthetic Learning: Learning through physical activities rather than listening to a lecture or presentation.

The workshop is uncomfortable for many, especially those with introverted tendencies, but it is low-risk. The extended metaphor of dance gives workshop participants a safe place to learn and practice both roles. If they have a preferred role, it pushes them to venture outside their comfort zones and take up a position they would not normally accept. For many people, it provides insight into both group dynamics and their own strengths while drawing light to areas for improvement.

This, of course, dovetails into another favorite comment of mine which was made by a staff member who had participated in a version of the workshop we had offered on campus.

"I have a new staff member I'm supervising and I keep getting feedback that I intimidate her," the woman explained. "But I just didn't see it. Until yesterday at the seminar. Yesterday, while I was leading, I saw that I could get pushy – literally. I saw the ways that I became impatient when my follower didn't get it. And I saw how hard it was to follow someone else's direction. I have to change the way I interact with my new employee. And with other people. I get it now. Thank you."

Leaders need willing followers to dance and work with. Followers need leaders who are able to communicate what needs to be accomplished clearly with empathy and understanding. Each needs the other to be competent and confident. Leadership is a partnership and the best partnership is created by two equally capable and self-assured partners who understand both halves of the whole.

Menial Tasks

Early in my career, I served for one year as Director of Alumni Services/Assistant Director of Development for a small, private college in Texas. One Friday afternoon, I found myself free and so decided to help the development staff prepare a large mailout. As I was working alongside the support staff stuffing envelopes and applying labels, one of the senior development directors strode through the office. Surprised and perhaps taken-aback seeing me there, he said, "Wow, Gage! It's good to see you can do menial labor too."

That fleeting comment made it painfully clear that he considered the work we were doing beneath him. This senior director couldn't imagine sitting down for a moment to support this dull, but crucial bit of work his employees were doing.

Even worse, instead of saying thank you or making a comment that recognized the importance of the task, he denigrated the work and the staff who were getting it done.

Understanding leadership as a partnership doesn't always mean sitting down and sharing someone's day-to-day work. It *does* mean appreciating the variety in complexity and the necessity of an enormous range of tasks needed for organizations to achieve their goals.

Leadership as a partnership requires leaders to understand they have time to concentrate on their projects because others are accomplishing the 'menial' tasks. It requires leaders to support, not merely direct others in their work. It means being willing to do all kinds of work when it is needed. You can't truly partner with someone if you look down on the work.

Reflection and Inventory

Circle the word that most aptly completes each sentence.
Take time to reflect on what you learn from your answers.

In my family, we talked about <u>leadership</u> _____.	Often Sometimes Rarely Never
When we discussed leadership, it was in a _____ light.	Positive Negative Not Applicable
In my family we talked about being a <u>follower</u> _____.	Often Sometimes Rarely Never
When we discussed being a follower, it was in a _____ light.	Positive Negative Not Applicable
In my current profession, I would identify myself as a _____.	Leader Follower
I was put in my current role as a leader or a follower _____.	Of my own accord or ambition Without a choice
I am happy with my current role as a leader or follower.	Yes Somewhat No

Lesson 2

Leading

"The only way to make sense out of change is to plunge into it, move with it, and join the dance."

Alan W. Watts

"Okay, take a step back with your left foot."

I do and he runs into me.

Thinking I didn't understand when to start, he counts out the beat. "Start with your left foot on one, okay?"

I do and again we crash.

My first lesson in the Texas Two-Step is not going well. I had moved to Lubbock two days prior and been invited by my new neighbor to go out dancing. I am on the crowded dance floor of an honest-to-goodness Texas dancehall with a man whom my gracious neighbor touts as a good dancer. As a teenager of the 70's, my dancing style at this point is to stand across from my partner and move separately. Any "partner dancing" we do is predominantly of the stand-and-sway variety, no matter the music accompanying it.

I am not prepared for the Texas Two-Step; I have no idea how to dance to Country and Western music, much less how to fix our uncoordinated movements. We stand there for a long moment being dodged by couples expertly whirling past us. I wonder if my new partner is going to give up on me. I wouldn't blame him.

Then, something seems to click for him.

"Oh wait, I'm starting on my left foot. You should be starting on your right foot."

Right there, I learn a fundamental dance lesson – people who aren't starting on the correct foot inevitably step on each other's toes.

Once we each start on the correct foot, everything falls into place. Although it isn't pretty or smooth, we are no longer a literal wreck. Even simple leadership tasks can be challenging.

Leading Is Difficult

Let's start by acknowledging that basic fact. Leading *is* difficult. On the dance floor and in organizations, leading takes skill, practice, and a willingness to take risks and open oneself to criticism. Working with others is challenging, whether a single partner on the dance floor or dozens of employees in a complex organization. In all arenas, leaders are expected to take care of the present, prepare for the future, and keep an eye on the wild and unpredictable antics of others. It's no wonder the expectations we have for leaders are often completely unrealistic.

I usually start the Leadership Dance workshop by asking people to gather in small groups of five or six participants with one person acting as a scribe. Then, I give them one minute to list every word that comes to mind when I say the word "leader."

Without looking at the example below, set a timer for one minute and create a list of words that you think best describes a leader.

What comes to mind when you hear the word "leader?"

Now, review your list. What do you notice?

If you are like most participants, you may have a name or two on your list, someone who embodies leadership for you. But most lists are filled with standard descriptors such as:

Courage	Commitment	Sense of Humor
Intelligent	Responsibility	Relationships
Trustworthiness	Reliability	Dependability
Self-Starter	Disruptive	Innovative
Forward-Thinker	Visionary	Model the Way
Troubleshooter	Communicator	Inspiring
Pro-Active	Collaborative	Bold
Excellence	Supportive	Skilled
Honest		

This is an actual list from a group of university administrators. It's a bit longer than most; I suspect their scribe was a fast writer. Leader Lists generally end up with 15 to 20 words depending on the dedication of the group and the speed of their designated scribe.

I invite each group to read its list. Group after group, workshop after workshop, Leader Lists are dominated by positive words, strong words, and words of inspiration. Rarely are negative words included. I point out this reality.

"Let's include 'Faster than a speeding bullet, more powerful than a locomotive, able to leap tall buildings in a single bound.' Anyone here able to do or be all of these things on these lists?"

Rueful smiles and head shakes spread across the room.

"We have high expectations for our leaders, don't we? I don't think I heard any negative words, or did I miss them?" Occasionally, I will have missed one, but generally, there aren't any. "No tyrant, no dictator, no bully. But there is a shadow side to leadership. People in power can abuse that power and can harm others, and we need to acknowledge that."

We spend time talking about people in leadership positions who are harmful, but the reality in our culture is that we usually see leadership as a positive trait, something to learn, something to aspire to. Although most of us have seen or experienced poor, if not actively malevolent management, when asked to define leadership as a whole, we trend toward the positive.

This matters for many reasons but for our purposes here, it means we often have unreasonable expectations for our leaders. And when they aren't able to meet those ideals, we feel as if we have been let down or that promises have been broken.

A Novice Leader

Technically, my first leadership positions were as vice-president for the French Club and president for the Speech and Drama club during my senior year in high school. I was elected because I was dependable; my peers knew I stayed on top of things.

In college, I was appointed secretary-general of the Oklahoma Model United Nations – because I was the only the candidate. I immediately began coordinating the work of 35 students who had been tasked with putting on a three-day conference for 500 college and high school students. Those were leadership roles but, in both cases, the safety net of advisors was strong.

In 1991, I was elected president of the Texas Association of College and University Student Personnel Administrators (TACUSPA). No safety net there. Deciding that TACUSPA was growing unwieldy and needed strategic reorganization, for my first board meeting as president we set up a two-day strategic-planning retreat.

The night before the board meeting, I slept restlessly and had repetitive dreams that left my head foggy and body sore come daylight. Clearly, I was stressed. Why had I ever thought bringing the board members onto a retreat would be a good idea? I didn't know anything about strategic planning; I was far outside my comfort zone.

Knowing I needed help, I reached out to a senior member of TACUSPA who specialized in strategic planning and organizational communication. I knew the organization well, but I didn't know the *steps*. No matter how passionate I was, my lack of knowledge and skill was limiting. I wanted to support my friends and colleagues across the state by ensuring TACUSPA would be around for the long-haul and asking for help from someone who knew how to dance was the key.

Who Can Lead?

Our unreasonable expectations about leadership feed into the idea that only a select few can be leaders. After all, as most participants in the Leadership Dance acknowledge, they can't meet the expectations they have listed let alone those of the broader society or even their own organization. Leading can be scary.

Of the three levels of ballroom dance – social, competition, and performance – social is the most difficult. It's an unexpected paradox for people unfamiliar with dancing. Performance dance, while intimidating for many, is the easiest. It is a set routine designed for a specific piece of music. The performers have practiced the routine continuously and the music provides known cues throughout the one to three minutes of the performance. While it's scary to be out there on your own in front of an audience, there's no one to get in your way. You have the floor and you can dance your dance.

For a competition, the dancers have also learned a routine, but they have no idea what song will be played. This means there are no cues in the music if they forget a step. Additionally, the floor will not be empty. In fact, in some situations, it might actually be quite crowded! Therefore, while the two dancers have practiced together and generally know the order of steps, the leader has to be able to pay attention to the other dancers on the floor, redirect their partner if someone is in the way, and lead new or modified steps smoothly.

In contrast, social dancing is all free form and, most often, on a crowded dance floor. Leaders have to pay attention to the music and the dancers on the floor, while planning what is to come next. They must lead each step clearly enough that their partners know what to do and are well-positioned to do it. There is a reason people are intimidated by leading on the dance floor. It is challenging and can be just plain hard even if you know the steps.

Positional leadership in organizations and communities is equivalent to social dancing. People who have titles that include the expectation of leadership such as president or vice president, chair or vice-chair, director, and principal to name a few, need to have the skills, knowledge, and abilities to meet the responsibilities they have taken on. They must simultaneously pay attention to numerous shifting factors, make decisions in real time, and communicate those decisions to diverse audiences without 'missing a beat.'

Now, imagine a dance floor with only one person leading and everyone else watching that person, waiting for cues and direction, trying to imagine what they are planning and thinking. It would be a mess, wouldn't it? That's often how we think about organizational leading. The person, or a limited number of persons, is designated as the leader and they are responsible for the success of everyone on the floor.

But positional leaders are not, or should not be, the only leaders in an organization or community. While there are comparatively few top leadership positions, the reality is that in healthy organizations, leadership should be happening throughout the organization. During Leadership Dance workshops, I have the positional leadership role as facilitator. I have set the direction for the dance and I start the music that holds us together, but the room is filled with leaders who have several responsibilities that they must fulfill for this workshop to work.

This is one of my most fundamental beliefs about leadership — all of us have the potential to be leaders. Some of us aspire to leadership;

some run from it. Some of us are coaxed into it while others come by the necessary skills innately.

Every person has lessons to learn along with skills and talents that need to be fostered and developed. Our competence as leaders is not determined by our ability to check off all of the items listed as leadership attributes at the start of this chapter. Our ability to lead is determined by our willingness to work on those skills and to take responsibility for improving something we care about.

What are your fundamental beliefs about leadership? Do they help you lead or hinder you?

Where did you learn about leadership? At school? In your first job? From a person? Elaborate.

What talents and skills do you have that support your style of leadership?

What skills do you need to learn or improve upon?

Where are you already leading despite not having a title?

Caring Equals Leading?

My understanding of leadership changed when I began to study and practice *servant leadership*. Robert K. Greenleaf coined the term and developed the philosophy in an essay published in 1970. However, even as late as the 1990's, the term was still relatively unknown.

One day while I was preparing for a class, a staff member dropped into my office. She looked at Greenleaf's book *The Power of Servant Leadership* resting on my desk and asked, "Isn't that an oxymoron?" She had never run across the term before. The idea of leadership as service to the organization and its members is a reversal of the expected power position of leadership.

Coincidentally, it was around that time when a student had stumped me with a rather simple question as we walked up the Student Union stairs together. "What exactly is your job? I mean, what do you do?"

My title was Associate Vice President and Dean of Student Life at Southern Methodist University (SMU), but to my chagrin, I didn't know how to answer her question. I guess I mumbled something before we parted ways, but it wasn't much of an answer. After some introspection however, I eventually distilled an explanation.

I realized my 'job' was to ensure SMU *worked* for the students who had chosen to come to that university. It was my job to make sure the university created systems, processes, programs, and conducive environments that gave students the opportunity to accomplish what they came to do. My job was to create space and opportunities for them to have those experiences.

Later, when I became a Vice President, I expanded my understanding of my work to include staff, faculty, parents, families, and the many constituents of the university. The purpose of my leadership was to serve all of them. And, of course, this included faculty and staff who deserved a healthy environment within which to work. They too should have opportunities to learn, grow, and achieve personal goals.

This revelation has been the focus of my leadership in one way or another for my entire career. But I certainly didn't know that when I started out. I didn't have leadership titles and I definitely didn't see myself as a leader even when others did. It was the former university president and leadership scholar Larraine Matusak who helped me understand this conundrum.

In her book *Finding Your Voice: Learning to Lead… Anywhere You Want to Make a Difference*, she states, "At some point in our lives, each of us has experienced that deep desire to make a difference, to be better than we are, to make our lives better at home or in our workplaces, to assume a leadership role in order to improve the situation for someone or some group in our community" (p. 3).

In other words, we find something we care about and we decide to act. It may be a small step, but our willingness to act – to make a difference – is the first step toward leading.

What do you care about?

Where do you want to make a difference?

What do you have the talent, energy, and willingness to do?

Practice, Practice, Practice.

It's the answer to an old joke – How do you get to Carnegie Hall? Practice, practice, practice. But that's also the answer to the question "How do I become a leader?" Although it's true that the start to leadership can be taking simple actions that make a difference, to be an effective leader on the dance floor and in your organization, whether you aspire to a title and position or not, you have to work at it. The only way to become a good leader is to practice leadership.

This book is just one of the multitudes out there on leadership; my own bookshelf contains several. The Leadership Dance isn't singular; there are countless other workshops and classes meant to instruct fledgling leaders. And there are skills to learn, ideas to reflect on, and information to gain from each of them. But to dance and to lead, we have to put the book down or leave the class and try. We have to make mistakes and learn from them. We have to accept that we won't meet expectations – our own and those of everyone around us. We have to act.

Just like my partner on that dance hall floor so long ago, we have to be willing to goof, crash into someone, and then stop to figure out what's going wrong. Yes, leading is difficult, but there is only one way to learn to lead – get on the dance floor and lead, lead, lead.

Pick a skill that leaders regularly use such as public speaking, running effective meetings, decision-making, delegation, or business writing and actively search for ways to improve upon it.

For example, if you find public speaking difficult, join ToastMasters International. If you are poor at constructing concise business memos, join an online group through Facebook or another social platform where you can receive critiques and advice from fellow leaders.

Lesson 3

Following

"Who dares to teach much never ceases to learn."

John Cotton Dana

There's a simple, undeniable reality in dance. It's not possible to lead someone who refuses to move their feet. The movie image of a leader whirling around the room dragging a limp partner in his arms – *Batman* (1989) with Jack Nicholson comes to mind, but there are others – isn't what most of us would call dancing. There's music and there's movement, but there isn't leading or following. It's certainly not dancing. Dancing, even at its most basic level, requires a willing follower. It works better with an able follower. It works best with a talented partner.

There are parallels in teaching. Teaching a room full of students who are staring at you with their arms crossed, literally or metaphorically, is hard work; not much is ever accomplished. I teach better with a room full of pupils who want to be there and who find the subject interesting; I suspect the same is true for most teachers. That's also my experience of leadership. Leaders who have an engaged group of followers enthusiastic about a goal or purpose are better leaders. And, of course, it's more exciting and fun when everyone is pulling together effectively toward a goal.

If I'm standing in front of a group of people and shout "Follow me!" and no one moves when I head toward the door, there's not a lot of leading going on. Even in instances of informal leadership, I can be working to make a difference in my organization, but if no one notices, if no one changes their own behavior, if I don't manage to create change or momentum, it's hard to call that leadership, isn't it? You might call me a good citizen of our organization, but I'm not a leader by most definitions. Leading requires following.

Following Is Difficult, Too.

Let's acknowledge that following is a skill every bit as much as leading though we rarely think of it that way. Like leading, following is challenging. Like leading, following comes more naturally to some, but it too is a skill that can be learned. Unfortunately, we rarely think of following as a skill or as important work and therefore, we rarely spend any time helping people learn to be effective followers.

The second activity of The Leadership Dance is designed to give participants a chance to ponder the concept of following. Just as we did with the Leader Lists, we split into small groups and, in the time span of one minute, come up with words to describe a follower.

Without looking at the example below, set a timer for one minute and create a list of words that you think best describes a follower.

What comes to mind when you hear the word "follower?"

Now, review this list. What do you notice?

I'll let you in on a secret. While I tell participants they have a minute to create a Leader List, I actually give them about 75 to 80 seconds.

When I reveal this during the discussion, participants are always surprised that they had more time for the second list. They are surprised because, with very rare exceptions, the Follower Lists are shorter, often significantly shorter, than the Leader Lists. Most groups report it was more challenging to think of words for the Follower List than for the Leader List.

Here is the Follower List from the same group as referenced in Chapter One.

Listener	Respect	Cautious
Trustworthy	Support	Cheerleader
Questioning	Inquisitive	Guarded
Team Player	Task-Oriented	Goal-Oriented

Twelve words compared to 25 and, except for the repetition of the word "trustworthy," a completely different list. This particular list had no negative words which, although unusual, is not surprising given that it was generated by college administrators who either have a more sophisticated view of leadership or are more practiced at censoring themselves. For some groups, the comparison is stark. The words aren't merely weaker but are quite negative. Groups that don't censor themselves and are willing to write down every word that comes to mind tend to include more derogatory terms like sheep, flunky, or servant.

As I often say in the workshop, "It shouldn't surprise you. After all, in our culture, leader equals good; follower, 'meh.' We sign up for classes in leadership, not followership." We need to rethink this cultural norm.

Who Can Follow?

You might be inclined to answer "Anyone," but the reality is that to follow well on the dance floor, followers have to do more than be willing to move their feet. To follow well in organizations, one has to do more than stay out of trouble. Good followers need skill every bit as much as good leaders do. Similar challenges can be found in the triad of performance, competition, and social dance discussed in the last chapter.

In a performance, for instance, both the leader and the follower have learned their individual steps. With many routines, they can practice without their partner. But even if they know their parts independently, leading and following must still happen when they dance together. It shows if they aren't actually working as a partnership. The dance isn't as smooth and the performance doesn't achieve perfection. In competition and social dancing, two people dancing independently can result in someone getting his or her toes stepped on at best. And on a really crowded dance floor, dance partners who aren't working together can get hurt or hurt someone around them.

Identify three examples of working as a leader with different followers. Review the details of those experiences.

Were you an effective leader for those particular partners? Why or why not?

How have you supported followers in learning and being effective in their roles?

Followers can't be sheep, simply relying on the leader to push them around the floor. They need to know what dance they are dancing;

they need to be willing to release control of the direction of the dance while still understanding their shared responsibility for the success of the venture. Followers need to be willing to share their thoughts and ideas while not taking over or "back leading," which means to lead as a follower – a major faux pas on the dance floor and a recipe for disaster.

Following takes finesse as well as simultaneous awareness of the leader and of everything that is happening on the dance floor. Great followers understand that there are times where they need to provide energy for the partnership, when they need to tell the leader of an impending collision, and when they can relax and enjoy the dance. Great followers make it possible for leaders to use their full abilities and for the duo to achieve the highest performance levels.

If you ever get a chance to watch a performance of the wildly popular television show "Dancing with the Stars" or a competition at your local ballroom dance studio, watch the different levels of dancing. At the local performance, pick an instructor or two and observe the difference in how they navigate the dance floor with their novice dancers as opposed to their advanced students. They look like completely different dancers, don't they? On "Dancing with the Stars," monitor the professional dancers with their star partners, especially at the beginning, then watch them dance with a professional partner. Here, the *dances* don't even look the same. No matter how talented a leader may be, they are only able to lead the steps their partner can follow. They may be able to help their partners flourish like my instructor did with me as described in the introduction, but the abilities of the followers still limit the scope of the dance.

All of this is equally true in an organization. Good followers need to be willing to engage their leaders (move their feet). Good followers need to understand the mission and the vision of the organization, to know its purpose (the dance). They need to understand how and when to be part of the decision-making process. Great followers aren't passive. Great followers don't wait to be told what to do. Great followers make it possible for leaders to imagine fantastic opportunities. Great followers are fully engaged members of their organizations and communities.

Unfortunately, we also seem to forget another reality. Most of us carry roles as followers while simultaneously acting as leaders to others. Vice Presidents report to Presidents. Presidents are responsible to their boards, stockholders, and other interested parties. Being a follower is a complex role in a dynamic situation. It is not for sheep.

Followers Care, Too.

It should come as no surprise that the best followers, like the best leaders, are working on something they care about. Many years ago, a colleague taught me an essential lesson about leading and following when he shared a simple phrase with me – work gets done where the energy flows. When you want something done, find people who have the energy for that idea, project, or task. In other words, find people who care.

I've worked to put that idea into practice whenever possible. Of course, we all have to complete tasks that we'd rather not spend time on. We do them because they are necessary to accomplish the higher goals of the organization and our work. But when it comes time for innovation, for making significant changes, for creativity, then absolutely look for the people who care.

Several years ago, I invited anyone in our division who wanted to work on student success to join me in a conversation. About 25 people showed up. Most of them didn't have senior leadership titles. By the end of the meeting, we had three work groups who had each taken on an idea they found interesting. All three groups went off for a couple of weeks, made time for further conversation around their day-to-day work, and came back to me with proposals.

We decided to try pilot programs for all three of the ideas. Each group received a small amount of seed money and went to work. All three ideas were reasonable and had the potential to make a difference for students on campus; additionally, all three groups had members interested in their particular projects.

As a follower, when have you worked with a great leader partner? What made them so effective?

But it was the group whose members were more than moderately interested, whose members genuinely cared about and believed in their idea, that gained enough traction to develop into a fully-funded project months later. There were multiple working parts to this group's plan which required engaging students and other staff members, but they made it work. Three years later, this program was going strong while the others had fallen by the wayside.

Followers Lead, Too.

While the official leaders of our division supported the pilot idea and agreed to allow staff members from their departments assume this extra responsibility, the work was accomplished by a wide variety of people from varying levels in the organization. Some might call them followers. But of course, they were leaders.

At the highest levels of dance, when both the leader and the follower really know what they are doing, the work of leading and following begins to shift. In the ordinary course of a basic dance, the leader provides the energy for the partnership. It is the leader's responsibility to make the first step that begins the dance. The leader, who is usually moving forward, determines the size, shape, and strength of the steps while considering the talents and skills of the follower. Eventually though, partners may dance in promenade (both facing forward) or in reverse positions with the leader facing backward.

In a beginner's dance with an inexperienced follower, the leader may still be providing the energy, pulling the follower forward. It's necessary and very awkward. But when there are two experienced partners, the energy shifts. Followers aren't pushed backward; they move on their own. In promenade, both partners contribute equal power. When the leader is moving backward, the follower's responsibility is to provide energy for the movement. The drive of the partnership ebbs, flows, and shifts according to the needs of the moment.

The same is true of organizational partnerships. While the formal leader may set the direction, the followers often need to provide the energy for getting the work done. No matter what title someone has, people who care become leaders. Followers and leaders work together as partners in an ever-changing dance. It's challenging to get right, but when it works, amazing things can happen.

Adams, Scott. "Dilbert Needs to Show Leadership." 22 December 2014. Accessed 11 Nov 2019. < https://dilbert.com/strip/2014-12-22>

Expectations and Experiences

Like leading, following takes practice. Becoming a great follower requires learning about and understanding your organization. Becoming a great follower means paying attention to what is happening around you, understanding what your leader is attempting to do, and figuring out what you can do to support that work.

Other Duties as Assigned

In 1985, McMurry College (now McMurry University) was a Methodist school of about 1,600 undergraduate students. During my third year as Assistant Dean of Students, I learned a valuable lesson about the power of being a follower. Sometime at the beginning of July, the Dean of Students departed on his traditional three weeks of vacation to his home in Connecticut. Although happy he was going to see family, I was apprehensive as things inevitably seemed to happen while he was away. The day after he left, our office received a phone call from the university's president.

In the center of the campus was a cul-de-sac that offered limited parking for visitors. Aside from the few meager spots available, the dead-end was comprised of fire lanes – which no one took seriously. The cul-de-sac was often lined with students' cars, something the president did not notice until that July morning. I was instructed to have all of the cars towed.

I disagreed with the President's decision as illegal parking was a common occurrence on this cul-de-sac and we had never before towed cars. Nevertheless, I sought out multiple towing companies and got quotes from them. As it turned out, because we were wanting to tow from private property, I had to contact the city police. Caught between a rock and a hard place, I decided to drag my feet to give the president time to cool off. I was certain he just needed to collect himself.

I met a police officer in the cul-de-sac that morning to discuss what should be done. By coincidence, the president of the university happened to be walking by, so I waved him over. I could see he was calmer, so I proceeded to explain to him the difficulties of towing the cars, concluding with the unfairness of an unannounced change of practice. I suggested ticketing each car; the president agreed providing I told each student they would be towed the next time.

And that is how I spent that hot July morning – standing with a police officer waiting for students to arrive at their cars so I could lecture them on illegal parking. I was an effective follower that day. I was able to resolve a sudden conflict by using my knowledge of my leader. I advocated for the students while navigating a difficult situation that could have led to community backlash. Knowing your dance partner is an important part of leading and following.

LEsson 4

BE Willing to LEad

"The one unbreakable rule of couple's dancing is that the partners must move interdependently, as a unit."

Gerald Jones

I've never actually been a dance teacher, but I have spent a lot of time in ballroom dance studios. From my perspective, one of the things dance studios do best is make it easy for their students to invite someone to dance. Ballroom dance students are often adults who have had negative experiences with dancing, but who are there to try again.

Dance studios are full of people who are learning, no matter how much dance experience they have. They know what it means to be a beginner, what it is to be frustrated when you just can't replicate what the instructor has demonstrated so easily, and therefore, tend to be supportive of everyone trying to learn. It's also the one place you are almost guaranteed to get a positive response to an invitation to dance, which is vital because deciding to lead is a risky venture.

Looking Like a Leader

Whether we like to admit it or not, some characteristics make it more likely we will view someone as a leader. We often hear the term "executive presence," meaning some mysterious way of holding oneself that commands respect. The term usually refers to specific characteristics – confidence, a strong speaking voice, an ability to command the room, extroversion. Unfortunately, this set of characteristics conjures a particular image in the United States – a tall, reasonably attractive white male is our archetype for leaders. Oh, and good hair doesn't hurt. While our ideas about leadership are beginning to morph, the reality is that in many organizations, people who don't fit this stereotype have to do more work to prove themselves.

This reality applies to both the dance floor and our organizational world. On the dance floor, people who are more attractive are more likely to get a positive response to their invitations to dance. But there is another factor beyond looks, presence, and stereotypes at play in this leadership interaction. Ability. In the world of ballroom dance, floor ability trumps the stereotype nearly every time, because if you are a dancer, the most fun you can have is with a really great partner. And that's even more true when you are the follower. If what you want to do is have fun dancing, looks don't matter.

The same is true in healthy organizations. We want to work with people who are great leaders. Once we get past our biases, what we really want is someone willing and able to lead effectively.

Willing to Lead

I've worked in complex organizations for more than 30 years. I've also worked on a variety of campuses as a consultant. Some of these organizations were small colleges; some were large universities that had the components of a mid-sized city, but they were all complex organizations. Regardless of size, however, the quality of leadership made a difference not only to the success of the organization, but to the people who were part of the organization.

I've also learned that some people in positions of leadership don't actually lead. They stand at podiums, make speeches and pronouncements, and – if the organization is lucky – develop strategic plans and vision statements. But they don't lead.

> What characteristics make someone a great leader to you?
>
> Has your understanding of who "looks like a leader" limited your understanding of who is truly an effective one?

Leadership is a complex activity because there are so many facets to it. It is leadership to focus internally and work to make the organization more functional. It is also leadership to work with community members, stakeholders, and outside constituents to help pave the way for future endeavors. It is leadership to manage quality by paying attention to details while designating and entrusting day-to-day tasks to others in the organization. In fact, there are a myriad of ways to be an effective leader, but they all share something in common.

I don't usually agree with everything I read in business books about leadership, but one concept I find absolutely true is the general phrase "It's about people, people, people." Leaders must be willing to engage the people of their organization. They have to be ready to support them in their jobs, their learning, and their leadership. Leaders need to be prepared to learn from their organizational members, to ask for their ideas, and to listen to them. Leaders must be willing to make unpopular, difficult decisions and be able to explain their reasons for the decision. Leaders have to hear and acknowledge the hard truths of the people working in their organizations. As leader and author Max De Pree writes in his 1989 book *Leadership is an Art*, "Leaders don't inflict pain; they bear pain" (p. 11). No wonder people, even people in leadership positions, opt out of authentic leadership.

I've seen people who are effective at many aspects of their job opt out of leadership responsibilities. They operate at the top level of their organization but don't take the time to do the difficult work of engaging their partners. They aren't actually "dancing" with people, but rather standing off to the side directing the flow of the work. It works for a while, but sooner or later a situation requires a deeper understanding of the organizational dynamics. When this happens and they aren't prepared to do the difficult work of leading, it is to the detriment of the organization and sometimes to themselves. We all need leaders who are willing to lead.

Conversation & Cupcakes

Part of "being willing to lead" is engaging with the members of your organization. If you don't engage or make yourself accessible, it's not possible to listen or learn from them, much less guide them. Engaging with your partners is relatively easy if you are leading a department of five or so colleagues, but becomes complicated with larger organizations.

Because engaging with countless employees is complicated, many busy leaders leave such responsibilities to departments heads thereby becoming distant figureheads to the people they are supposed to be leading. When I became Dean of Students, one of the first things I did was have a meeting with everyone in the departments who reported to me.

Shortly after the notice went out, Donna, who had been the Dean's assistant for a long time, came to check with me. "I'm getting calls from people who want to be sure – do you mean *everyone* is invited?" Yes, I did. But apparently that was so unusual for this group of departments that multiple people felt the need to confirm their understanding.

That first meeting became a commonplace practice for me when entering new leadership positions. It's not only a way to help people learn more about who I am and what I care about, but it helps familiarize them with my expectations and values. I take a litany of questions, including ones colleagues weren't allowed to ask during the interview.

That's a great start, but it's not enough. Every leader needs to find ways to engage and stay that way. Social media can help, but it's not enough. A regular newsletter can help, but it's not enough. Though I have to say I've found both of these to be very effective in different ways for different people, by themselves they *aren't enough*.

Being willing to lead takes interaction. No, in large organizations we can't meet, let alone spend time with everyone, but we have to open ourselves up to interaction as often, in as many ways, and as many places as possible. Here are a few quick examples that have been successful for me:

- Hold large meetings at critical times
- Attend small departmental meetings
- Celebrate successes and individuals.
- Attend events put on by staff to see the results of their hard work
- Invite people to informal small-group gatherings for conversation and cupcakes to celebrate birthday months or anniversary dates

Leading with Clarity

There are many ways to ask someone to dance. There's the classic, "Hey, ya wanna dance?" Often directed at an entire table, it's mushy and unclear. But the reality is, even if clearly directed to a specific person, a polite but general "Would you like to dance?" isn't always helpful.

One evening while visiting a dance studio for lessons, I found myself sitting next to a new student. After watching the dance floor crowded with couples, the new student leaned over and asked, "What dance is this?" I scanned the people before me and then frowned. No wonder she was confused. While the music had a lively tempo and strong beat, it lent itself to multiple dances, at least three of which were being demonstrated on the floor. If I'm the follower and which dance we're going to be dancing matters to me, a general invitation isn't much help.

The best invitation to dance is clearly directed to one person and makes a specific request. "Would you like to do the swing?" It saves the embarrassment of misunderstanding which person has been invited. Additionally, if I'm not interested in doing or able to do that particular dance, I can not only politely refuse, but can also explain why. This allows the leader to walk away, change the invitation, or even offer to help the follower learn.

Once on the dance floor, the leader's ability to lead clearly is critical. When the leader's signals, movements, and leads are clear and confident, it makes it possible for the partner to follow complicated moves and patterns smoothly and gracefully.

We generally want our most senior leaders to have a vision for the future, a goal for the entire organization to work toward. To continue the dance metaphor, we want leaders who know what dance they are leading and which direction to move on the floor. We want and need leaders to have clarity of purpose, to be able to articulate why our work is important, and what we need to do to get there. A positional leader who can't do this squanders the trust of the organization's members.

Of course, there are multiple ways of developing that vision. It is possible for leaders to decide on the vision and direction on their own. They are in the position to choose, and they can and often do. And usually, as long as they are staying within the general parameters of the organization's purpose, this choice is theirs to make. This style can be reassuring as it is simple and clear. The leader has the responsibility; it's the job of the followers to do their work. Conversely, it can be very frustrating if the leader is addicted to always wanting to try the new thing, the next big idea with the result that the work is always changing.

Understanding leadership as a partnership suggests a different approach to developing a vision. This version however, is not only less straightforward, but takes longer. Leadership as a partnership asks leaders to involve their partners to foster a shared vision. It requires asking difficult questions and taking the time to listen deeply to the answers, especially the uncomfortable ones. It requires inviting everyone into the conversation AND taking their voices and views into consideration.

For many organizations, it will require teaching people how to reimagine new ways of carrying out their duties, envisioning different futures, and, even more complicated, letting go of useless habits or no-longer-applicable processes. Once this challenging work is completed, there's a better chance that everyone in the organization will understand the vision and therefore understand how their own work contributes to that vision and purpose. That's leading with clarity.

Leading with clarity creates the opportunity for leadership to develop throughout the organization. When everyone is moving in the same direction and understands the overall purpose, it becomes possible for individuals to be creative, to develop their own style of leading within their areas of responsibility and expertise, and to find ways to move the organization toward the vision without specific direction from "above."

It's certainly possible to push a metaphor too far; after all, the movement on a dance floor is typically circular, not forward. But on the dance floor, the general movement is in the same direction. All of the leaders have a wide-ranging idea of what needs to be accomplished – say, a waltz – and they know they need to circle the floor in the same way. With those guidelines, however, leaders have full choice based on their skills and those of their partners to dance the waltz in their own style. It may be large and flowing, or, for a beginner, small and boxy. No matter what though, it's still a waltz, and it is still part of the overall movement of the group.

What does clarity in organizational leadership mean to you?

Have you experienced the equivalent of a muddled invitation to be part of an organizational effort? What was that experience like?

What about the opposite? What does clear leadership in your organization look like?

Lesson 5

Lead with Finesse

"Lesser dancers stumble; better dancers syncopate."

Unknown

You can often spot pushy leaders on the dance floor. The country-and-western version often includes the leader with an arm around his partner's neck. I choose not to dance with people who use that style because the leader can't help but pull you around by your head, especially if you are shorter in stature like myself. I suspect some leaders like the style for that reason.

But even when a leader dances with the usual lead of the right hand on the shoulder blade, you can see people who are pushing their partners around. Trust me; it's not fun for the partners and neither of the choices for a subsequent response work particularly well.

If you just let it happen, your right arm gets pushed into an odd and uncomfortable position and your toes get stepped on because you don't get out of the way fast enough. If you counteract by trying to match the leader's strength, it becomes a taxing exercise. It can even devolve into a power struggle with each partner trying to take control. If only such leaders could relax a bit and try for finesse and grace instead of muscle, they might find dancing more fun and interesting for them and their partner.

Being Pushy

We've already discussed some of the reasons leading is difficult. Finding the right amount of strength to use is another one of those challenges. Let's start with examples from the Leadership Dance workshop.

When followers have a chance to comment on their various leaders, a frequently mentioned statement is that some leaders are pushy. Because it is a leadership workshop rather than a dance class, I don't ask them to use a traditional dance hold. For many people, that's just too much like holding hands with their colleagues. To minimize discomfort, I ask participants to bring their hands to shoulder level with their palms facing forward and then touch palm-to-palm. Even that is a bit much for some people.

This palm-to-palm technique, however, helps participants navigate gender norms while emphasizing leadership. I have had some men – yes, it's always men – who choose to dance without using their hands when paired with another male. College-age students rarely have trouble with the concept. For the most part though, participants see handholding as part of this already awkward experience and after a few nervous laughs, go along with it.

The purpose of this special handhold is twofold. Not only does it keep tense and uncomfortable people from squeezing their partners' hands, but it makes it easy to spot forceful leaders. If a partner's hands are pushed past the mid-point between the dancers, the follower may be leaning back to cope with the leader's vigorous navigation.

Conversely, when pushy leaders are moving backward, they often leave their partners an entire pace behind. To be fair, this handhold is not a good one to use for moves where the leader moves backward. Nevertheless, it's an example of the reality that pushy leaders are often entirely focused on their own role, determined to lead with a capital "L," and unaware of the reactions and experiences of their partners. It can be a miserable experience for the follower and it's not particularly effective for a leader who wants to be successful.

Where have you seen a pushy leader? What behaviors did they exhibit that led you to conclude they were pushy?

Have you been told you're a pushy leader, too aggressive, or intimidating? What behaviors or attitudes do you think lead to such feedback?

Then there are the leaders we love to dance with. Their style of leading might be soft or firm, but it's clear, easy to understand, and simple to follow. They may not know a lot of steps, but they know how to lead the steps in their repertoire well. They lead with finesse.

Leading a dance well is a skill anyone can learn, but there's one attribute that truly wonderful leaders have. They are acutely attuned to the skills, talents, and reactions of their partners. They notice which leads work and which do not. Furthermore, they quickly grasp when their partner doesn't understand what they are trying to lead and adjust accordingly. When such leaders realize that a step or pattern is unfamiliar, they make a shift and match their leads to the skill and knowledge of their partner smoothly and without comment. They make dancing fun!

Syncopation

"Lesser dancers stumble; better dancers syncopate," reads the quote at the beginning of this chapter. Syncopation in dance means the ability to dance more steps than there are beats. So, if there are two beats and you dance three steps in a triplet, you've completed a syncopation.

While dancing the Merengue, dancers step on every beat. One, two, three, four is left, right, left, right. It's very simple. When you are an inexperienced dancer, a stumble can mean that you will have to wait for the next downbeat so you can properly begin once more on the left foot. But a more experienced dancer understands that music syncopates and, by adding an extra step or two to make up for the mistake, they can correct the error instead of fully stopping.

It's leading with finesse. All of us make mistakes in our work and in our leadership. The ability to recover from those mistakes takes time to cultivate just as finding the rhythm in a difficult piece of music can be challenging. Leaders who have a deep understanding of both the purpose of an organization and the work they are doing can recover from mistakes quicker and more smoothly.

Leading with Finesse

Wait, I hear you saying, "We need strong leaders! Didn't you just say we need more people to lead, to actually take charge?" Absolutely, we do need strong leaders, but there's a difference between being strong and being imperious. Off the dance floor, we call those leaders bullies.

Have you ever worked with a leader who is a bully? Bullies come in all shapes and sizes. Some can be loud and obnoxious leaders who browbeat their people to ensure staff members are doing what they're supposed to be doing; others can be micromanagers who check employees' work continuously, never trusting that they can accomplish the requisite tasks. They can manipulate their employees by assigning and withholding rewards and praise according to today's whim. There is no shortage of bullies in the workplace.

In my opinion, bully organizational leaders and pushy dance leaders possess two prevailing traits – a lack of confidence in their own abilities to lead and an inability to empathize with their partners. Dancers who are uncertain about their knowledge and skills often overcompensate by pushing their partners around the floor. They may be pulling on an arm, squeezing a hand too tightly, or using more muscle than is necessary. Similarly, leaders in organizations who are not confident in their skills often bluster, yell, or belittle others to hide their unease. When leaders are unable to empathize with their partners, neither understands nor cares about the effects of their strong-arming techniques.

One skill missing here is communication. On the dance floor, communication occurs in a variety of ways. During the Leadership Dance workshop, it may be as simple as the leader saying to the partner, "Left, right, forward, backward" or "We're going to go backward eight steps now." It can be more subtle, perhaps a nod of the head, a motion of the hand, or a definitive step in one direction or another. But clarity is what matters and paying attention to how partners respond teaches leaders how effective their communication methods are. It's clear from watching the dance, leaders who find ways to clearly communicate expectations and what comes next are more fun to dance with – fewer toes are injured in the process.

In organizations, one of the most common complaints from members is the lack of communication from leaders. It may be about matters as large and complex as vision and direction, but it may also be what success looks like for a specific task. Leaders who don't communicate effectively across their organizations step on a lot of toes. They also grow frustrated when their organizations fail or don't function as expected.

Conversely, leaders who take the time to find multiple ways to share what they consider essential find their partners are more likely to understand how their work fits into the larger vision. Their partners then make better decisions, tend to take the initiative, and be more effective.

Have you ever worked with an organizational leader who has the finesse of a great dance partner? Such a leader has a clear idea of the organization's purpose and an understanding of what it takes to accomplish that purpose – in other words, they know what the dance is and how to dance it! Such a leader can communicate this information to the members of the organization clearly, and in the best situations, in a way that inspires everyone to do their finest work in accomplishing this purpose.

When a leader is new to the dance, to the task, or to leading in general, communication becomes even more critical. New leaders who are willing to ask questions, seek feedback, and learn are ultimately more effective in their work. A leader with finesse can imagine what a significant change will mean for staff members and will work to address concerns when possible. Leaders with finesse have empathy and work to lead and communicate in a way that is most effective for their partners.

Least Amount of Force

Several years ago, I made a faculty member mad. While I don't remember the exact details, the situation involved a case of cheating that had occurred in his class and the subsequent retaliatory responses.

Some faculty members regard cheating in the classroom as a personal affront and believe offenders should be kicked out of school for violations of academic integrity. Others believe students should get a chance to learn from their mistakes and don't wish for consequences to be unnecessarily harsh.

At the time of the disagreement, I was the Assistant Dean for the conduct office at The University of Texas at Austin. The faculty member had brought the problem to my attention initially by phone and then by notes and emails – which was acceptable. It wasn't until the faculty member continued to submit constant, personalized notes and emails in an increasingly hostile tone that it became a problem. In fact, the frequency and tone of the written messages were so troubling, it borderlined workplace harassment.

Growing concerned, the Dean of Students and I discussed our next course of action with the dean of the faculty member's college. He suggested having a well-respected member of the college faculty reach out to the disgruntled colleague. Thankfully, that conversation convinced the professor to desist and that was the end of the matter.

That is the epitome of leading with finesse. The Dean of the College listened to and acknowledged my concerns and then, like an experienced dancer, applied the least amount of force necessary to help his follower move in the right direction.

Skills Related to Managerial Success & Leading with Finesse

Resourcefulness	Can think strategically, engage in flexible problem solving, and work effectively with higher management.
Doing whatever it takes	Has perseverance and focus in the face of obstacles.
Being a quick study	Quickly masters new technical and business knowledge.
Building and mending relationships	Knows how to build and maintain working relationships with co-workers and external parties.
Leading subordinates	Delegates to subordinates effectively, broadens their opportunities, and acts with fairness toward them.
Compassion and sensitivity	Shows genuine interest in others and sensitivity of subordinates' needs.
Straightforwardness and composure	Is honorable and steadfast.
Setting a developmental climate	Provides a challenging climate to encourage subordinates' development.
Confronting problem subordinates	Acts decisively and fairly when dealing with problem subordinates.
Team orientation	Accomplishes tasks through managing others.
Balance between personal life and work	Balances work priorities with personal life so that neither is neglected.
Decisiveness	Prefers quick and approximate actions to slow and precise ones in many management situations.

Self-awareness	Has an accurate picture of strengths and weaknesses and is willing to improve.
Hiring talented staff	Hires talented people for the team.
Putting people at ease	Displays warmth and a good sense of humor.
Acting with flexibility	Can behave in ways that are often seen as opposites.

Directly sourced from: Noe, Raymond A., John R. Hollenbeck, Barry Gerhart, & Patrick M. Wright. (2010). Employee development. *Human Resource Management: Gaining a Competitive Advantage* (7th ed., pp. 424). New York, NY: McGraw-Hill/Irwin.

What Does It Mean to Be a Strong Leader?

Leading with finesse is not a weak style. It's not wishy-washy. On the dance floor, a wishy-washy leader is frustrating and difficult to dance with. In dance, some leaders have very firm leads and others, who are just as effective, have light, subtle leads. But effective light leads are not weak or indecisive just as the firm style isn't pushy or overbearing. Both styles can be very effective when used correctly.

As with everything else, we each have preferences, but for myself, I want to dance with someone who is clear about what they are doing and is able to make sure I know what is expected of me. In the best of all worlds, the leader ensures I'm in the best place possible to succeed. In an organization, it means precisely the same thing.

> Think about the leaders you know in your organizations and communities. What leaders do you know who lead with finesse?
>
> What do you see, feel, or hear that makes you categorize them this way?

Some leaders have an extroverted, exuberant style. They are upbeat, excited, and full of energy. Others are more reflective, preferring small-group interactions. They are also enthusiastic and fervent, but might not express it in the same way. Both styles can be equally effective. Some leaders observe organizational happenings at a macroscale while others like to delve into the details – though not in a micromanaging sense. No matter where leaders land along the spectrum, they can still be engaged leaders who set their partners up for success rather than push them into compliance.

We do need strong leaders. We need people who are willing to do the hard work of leadership. We need leaders who are strong enough to know their followers are capable of being great dance partners and need support rather than direction.

We need dynamic leaders who are willing to engage their partners and rally their variety of skills, talents, and styles for the good of the partnership and organization. We need leaders who listen and who communicate clearly and concisely; we need leaders who can empathize. We need leaders with finesse who work with us to accomplish amazing things.

> Look at your own leadership. Are there places and times when you believe you led with finesse? What did you do or say that leads you to this assessment? Be specific.
>
> What were the circumstances?
>
> Who were the people?
>
> How much did those circumstances and people play a part in you being a smooth leader?

LESSON 6

Dance to the Music

"Those who were seen dancing were thought to be insane by those who could not hear the music."

Friedrich Nietzsche

One morning as I was facilitating a workshop for a staff group, the most skeptical participant in the room asked me a question I had yet to encounter. It's not unheard of for a participant in the Leadership Dance to ask me a new question, but after so many sessions, it's typically more a matter of new details than different questions. This one, however, was unexpected.

As we neared the end of the workshop, most of the participants had gained enough confidence in the patterns and their roles to explore a bit. The skeptical participant, a young woman, approached me and asked in a somewhat challenging tone, "So, I have a question. It's easier to dance the pattern, to stay together with my partner when the music is playing. Is there something equivalent to the music for our organizational work?"

Everyone fell silent to hear my response. After a moment's thought, I said, "That is an interesting question and a new one. It's the organization's vision and mission. It seems to me the reason it's easier to dance with music is that the music provides a framework that supports and structures the dance. Done well, that's what the vision and mission do for an organization. They provide a framework and a structure. They help everyone find his or her own rhythm and direction. They help give the work shape, form, and purpose just as music does for a dance."

My on-the-spot explanation must have made sense to my skeptical participant because she nodded and went right back to the dance. In the subsequent exercise – working on vision and mission statements – she appeared more enthusiastic and in a more positive mindset.

Clear, concise vision and mission statements provide structure and support for the work that we do. They help us be better leaders.

Understanding the Music

For all of the music I have loved in my life, I don't know that I ever really understood its structure until I was immersed in ballroom dance. I mean, of course I could count a beat. I could hear the difference between a waltz, rumba, or cha-cha, but it turned out that there was more going on than I knew.

It was during a ballroom dance workshop that a coach took the time to teach us about the internal structure and makeup of the music to which we danced. Music on the radio isn't just a repetition of four beats – or three for a waltz. There are phrases, paragraphs (though no one uses that term), and discrete sections within a song.

Ballroom Guide puts it this way:

Individual beats group together to make a bar (aka a measure). For example, Cha-Cha, Rumba, Jive, Foxtrot, and Quickstep all have four beats per bar. These bars group together to make phrases. Typically, there are eight bars per phrase. These phrases then group together to make a full piece of music. Beginner dancers learn to pay attention to when the beats come, but more advanced dancers need to learn to pay attention to the bars and phrases because not all bars of music are the same. Making your dancing fit not only the beats but also the differences among the bars of music is called phrasing.

Ballroom Guide. (2016 March 16). Musicality and Phrasing [Web log post. Accessed December 9, 2019. http://www.ballroomguide.com/resources/blog/2016_03_14_musicality_and_phrasing.html>

For the average dancer on the social dance floor, staying on beat is the most critical action. As you advance as a dancer, however, you must be able to hear and intuit the internal workings of a song to allow your dancing to flourish and grow. Skills such as knowing when a chorus is transitioning, when a phrase will end, or even when a piece's time signature will change are considered advanced in ballroom dance. Developing an awareness of the internal phrasing can help you add finesse to your dance and unlock more complicated and intuitive patterns.

Similarly, comprehension of the internal purpose and a thorough understanding of the vision and mission of your organization are the foundations of leadership.

Can you recite the vision or mission statement of any organization you've been a part of?

If not, can you at least succinctly explain its purpose?

Leading to the Music

The first step in any activity, of course, is understanding your objective. On the dance floor, knowing what dance you are leading matters. In an organization, leaders need to know what they are trying to achieve. I always give credit to Simon Sinek, the author of *Start with Why: How Great Leaders Inspire Everyone to Take Action*, for this idea because he did the Technology, Entertainment, Design (TED) Talk to which I often refer, but I figured out a version of this for myself when I became Vice President of Student Affairs at The University of Texas at San Antonio. It was then that I came to understand part of my job as a leader was to help everyone understand the music that gave our dance structure.

I had moved from a small organization of about five departments and 50 people to one of 19 departments and approximately 450 people. It wasn't the first time I found myself supervising areas in which I had no expertise, but it was the first time I had supervised such a large collection of departments performing such a wide variety of functions all at once.

In my previous position at the smaller school, health services had reported to me, but the department was staffed by five nurses and a part-time doctor with a limited scope of service. Now, health services consisted of about 25 people offering an extensive range of services, all of which came with varying inherent risks. Additionally, the university's NCAA Division I Intercollegiate Athletics program reported to me. It was painfully clear I had to adjust my understanding of leading this diverse group of people and functions.

I would never be an expert in most of what we did. I would not be able to - nor should I – try to set the direction for the future of many of the departments in our division. The leaders of the individual departments needed to do that.

Then, what was my role as a leader? Simple, really. I needed to keep the music going and make sure as many people as possible knew how to dance to that music. To do this, I had two main tasks. First, it was my responsibility to clearly and concisely state our "why," to use Sinek's terms. While the department heads determined the "what," I set the "why." In other words, it was my job to ensure the organization's purpose, our reason for work, was being conveyed effectively to the staff. Our vision and mission statements needed to reflect the future and current states of that purpose.

Second, not only was I to address the "why," but I was to always be clear about the "how" – the manner in which we should work to collectively accomplish the larger purpose. Our values and procedures needed to provide clear guidance to everyone about the way we delivered services and interacted. I was responsible for articulating those values and my expectations as the leader of this division while modeling, encouraging, and reinforcing these practices.

How closely do the actions of your organization match those stated in its mission statement or vision?

What Music Do You Dance to?

The purpose should vary from organization to organization. Not every organization we work for in a career will have the same purpose. However, I suspect that most organizations you have liked working for have had similar lived values. I know that as I have advanced in my career, the values I lead from have not shifted significantly over time. Oh, I've learned and grown; some details have changed and my ability to identify and articulate what is important to me has improved, but the basics – what I care about and the values that are important to me – haven't changed.

I value collaboration over competition; I support people working across organizational lines. I believe creativity is critical and have worked to support innovation within organizations. I expect people to understand the purpose, the vision, and the mission and to use that understanding to guide their work. I set high standards, work to help people achieve them, and hold them accountable when they don't. And I value and support leaders and the development of leadership throughout the organization.

When deciding whether to join an organization, I look for the "music." What is the organization's purpose? What is the organization trying to accomplish? What are the values that guide its work? Does that work match the organization's purpose and stated values? Does any of it match *my* values and beliefs?

Over time, I have improved in my ability to lead, to dance to the music. I have learned the hard way that leaders must clearly articulate their expectations, even ones that seem basic, because not everyone has the same background and experiences. My ability to lead has improved as I have become more skilled at sharing, teaching, and modeling the fundamental elements of our organizational culture (the music) – the why and the how. I hold meetings and talk about my expectations. I write newsletter articles to share stories of meaning and purpose. I engage staff when considering matters that are important to me and issues that are important to them. In other words, I work to ensure we are all dancing to the same music and that we all understand the structure of the music and our work. When more people dance well to the music, the entire experience becomes enjoyable. Subsequently, we become more effective as a group in living our mission and achieving our purpose.

Turn the Volume Up

It was many years before I came to know this fact and realize the power behind a leader leading with a mission in mind.

One of the best leaders I ever worked with was the former president of The University of Texas at San Antonio (UTSA). A historian who made his points through stories and metaphors, he was a non-traditional leader who often frustrated people accustomed to strict directives and numbers-based initiatives. He held weekly cabinet meetings for those immediately working under him during which his most recent conversations with leaders around the university, the city, and state, as well as campus initiatives from divisions and colleges were discussed.

Because he had set clear goals – transform UTSA from a commuter school to a dynamic, academically vibrant campus-of-choice – we knew the direction in which we needed to head. As we talked and discussed the issues certain departments were spearheading, the mission he had set before us solidified.

Even without referring to the mission statement, our assignment was set. The president made sure we could hear the music – and we certainly learned to dance well!

Lesson 7

Be Worthy of Trust

"The first job of any leader is to inspire trust. Trust is confidence born of two dimensions: character and competence. Character includes your integrity, motive, and intent with people. Competence includes your capabilities, skills, results, and track record. Both dimensions are vital."

Stephen Covey

At the beginning of the Leadership Dance workshop, I ask participants to take four steps to the left or right depending on their place in the circles. This, of course, leads to a round of confusion and uncoordinated movements. Some people, not understanding that each move of a foot counts as a step, take eight steps. Others take huge strides regardless of how much room there is around them while a creative few do a crossover step that looks like they are performing an agility drill at football practice.

After some awkward laughter and clarifying instructions, everyone figures out what they need to do. Immediately thereafter, I ask them to move to expand and contract the circles. In other words, walk four steps backward and four forward. Suddenly, participants start doing the wedding march – leading with one foot while bringing the other up stiffly before taking the next step – instead of simply walking backward and forward. Asking people to dance seems to encourage them to be fancy.

Competence

Perhaps, though, it's the anxiety of doing something unfamiliar, something they aren't sure how to do. Half of the participants are being asked to lead a partner in an awkward, unknown activity, after all. The other dancers are expected to follow leaders who may or may not be at all comfortable performing such a task so soon after learning it.

It's not surprising that it all goes a bit wonky in the beginning. It's one of the first discussions most workshop participants have. Followers talk about the difference between following leaders who understand the steps and those who do not. As you would expect, it's easier to follow someone who has at least a basic grasp of the task at hand. Leaders who concentrate exclusively on moving their feet rarely do an effective job of connecting with or communicating with their partners. There's a reason dance instructors admonish students for looking at their feet. Actually, there are two – looking down not only puts you off balance, but it makes it nearly impossible to communicate with your partner.

Off the dance floor, leaders need to pay attention to more than the mechanics of leading the immediate task. In organizations, competency will get you started while you learn to lead, but it's not enough to be an effective leader. Yet, as on the dance floor, skill at leading can mitigate the challenges of not knowing the details of the task.

During the workshop, participants often mention their increasing competence as they move from one round to the next. As they become more experienced, their ability to lead the dance increases. In addition, their partnerships become smoother and the dance more fun. The same is true in organizations. It's much better to work for a competent leader than someone who doesn't know how to lead.

At this point in the workshop, we usually spend some time discussing the organizational experience of working with a new leader. Even if the individual coming in has a great deal of experience in the task to be done, there is a learning curve related to doing that task with new partners in a different configuration. And if the person is new at leading, there is even more to learn. It's no wonder things can get a bit wonky during leadership transitions in our organizations.

Situational leadership theory teaches leaders a way to respond to the needs of their followers by analyzing their maturity (knowledge and ability) in relation to the task at hand. But there is a situational reality for leaders, too. The ability of a leader to be effective in the role is connected to their competency in both the task to be accomplished and their level of skill as a leader.

Think about the times you have been a new leader. Perhaps you were new to leadership as a whole, or new to a position, or even new to a task put in your charge.

How would you rate your competence? How did your competence or lack thereof influence your efficacy as a leader?

As a subordinate, have you ever experienced or witnessed a fledgling leader? How would you describe their competence?

Confidence

In the workshop, while the participants who started as followers have it somewhat easier, when it is their turn to lead, the first thing they must do is make a significant mental shift. They also have to change feet. Followers start with the right foot and take their first step to their right; leaders start with the left foot and move left. For followers moving into leader roles, this, of course, becomes reversed, but after a moment's practice, most people are capable of making the change. Obviously, making the move from team member to leader in an organization is not so simple.

The leaders for the next three rounds already know the primary task. The relative simplicity of making this switch is one of the reasons I teach the Merengue. After completing three rounds as followers, these leaders know the dance steps. And it shows. Subsequent rounds go more smoothly than the initial three. The participants are more relaxed, laughter comes readily, and the energy in the room is higher during the second set.

Throughout the first three rounds, I have given the instruction "Dance the pattern (left, right, forward, backward) twice and then you're on your own." It is rare for a leader to break the pattern in the first two rounds, though it does happen, especially when an individual loves to dance. I remind my participants, "No turns, no spins, no dips, no lifts," advice designed both to get a laugh and to maintain some level of control. Even with those limitations, there's still a lot they can do. However, most leaders are so focused on doing their four steps, they can't imagine doing anything else. So, I give them a hint.

"You can take eight steps backward or forwards to break out of the circle. Then you can choose any direction. Take steps in sets of four and you'll be fine."

On round three, a few adventurous souls break out of the pattern and head for the far corners of the room where they have more space.

When we switch roles, the majority of the new leaders stick with the pattern for round one, but there are a few who break the pattern as soon as they have permission. They want to try something new to test their ability to lead. Their competence in the basic steps gives them the confidence to do something more.

By the fifth round, nearly everyone finds it possible to dance "on their own." At this point in the workshop, the energy level in the room begins to change. Faces and shoulders are visibly more relaxed; the leaders have more competence and confidence and, as a result, are better at using their influence. Their followers are more capable as well, finding it easier to try new patterns. In fact, the followers are now working with leaders who lead reasonably well and can keep them out of harm's way, which means they are more willing to try new things. And everyone's dancing reaches new levels.

During your leadership, you inevitably experienced times of uncertainty.

Did you hide your concerns or questions? Did you ask for help or guidance? How did your indecisiveness affect the people you were leading?

Inspiring Trust

Of course, a leader can become over-confident. Sometimes this happens because leaders overestimate their skill level in either the task or their ability to lead. On the dance floor, this can happen to a leader who was quite comfortable with the dance steps while walking through them alone, but finds that working with a partner adds a new and complicating set of variables. In organizations, a promotion requires a shift from peer to leader and the task expert suddenly flounders. Or a new person comes into an organization and finds that his or her "moves" are no longer quite so smooth; their cues aren't immediately understood.

In these situations, leaders have a difficult choice. Some double down; since a style or behavior worked before, they are sure it will work again. Others try to adjust on the fly. And a radical few stop and re-think their strategies.

During the Leadership Dance, most people seem to be willing to admit their confusion, ask for and accept help, and try again. With a bit of guidance from a willing partner, most people begin to be more successful. It's a strategy we should all be willing to try. Unfortunately, in our organizations, many, if not most, leaders seem to have difficulty with being perceived as other than infallible.

Toward the end of the workshop, I ask for a volunteer. I ask them to let me lead, keep their arms loose, and keep their feet marching. After a few practice steps, when we are in sync, I lead them in a moderately complex set of turns and pretzel-y maneuvers ending with them ducking under my arm. And it works just fine. Not always perfect. Some people need a bit more coaching as we go, but we always accomplish the task well enough to earn a round of applause. Then I ask the group, "Why did that work?"

Answers include, but are not limited to: "Because you know what you are doing" and "Because she's willing to follow." Both are true, but eventually, we get to the response I'm seeking – "Because she trusted you." I add this little bit of fun because we often arrive at the end of the workshop without having discussed the issue of trust. I think it doesn't come up because the task is simple and, while it is uncomfortable for some people, it's ultimately low-risk. Their trust is not in their dance partners at that point. It's in me as the teacher/facilitator.

But the bit of dance I lead asks the follower to do something they haven't been taught or prepared to do. The volunteers are standing in the middle of a circle of their peers and they have no idea what is going to happen. They have good reason to be anxious. And yet, we manage to dance because my partners are willing to trust me, trust that I'm not going to embarrass or hurt them, trust that I know enough to untangle us, trust that my confidence in both our abilities is not misplaced. I've earned that trust over the past hour and a half.

Trust is a critical component of the leadership partnership. Although followers need to be trustworthy too, leaders have the responsibility first and foremost. This brings us to the second part of the equation – character. Not only must leaders be competent, they must also be people of character. They need to be honest, ethical, and appropriately confident while possessing a level of self-awareness of their abilities. Capable, trustworthy leaders don't bluster and fake their way through. They don't double down on an unsuccessful strategy. Effective, reliable leaders are confident enough to admit when they don't have answers, ask for help and support, and learn to do better.

How have confidence, competence, and trust factored into your leadership experiences?

What have you learned from others that helped you inspire trust?

When have you been seen as a trustworthy leader and why?

Leading with Integrity

During the last 20 minutes or so of the Leadership Dance, I teach the group a basic underarm turn. It's a simple maneuver; leaders lift their left arms straight up and followers turn in place under the archway. Everyone practices and then I stop the group. As is true of many parts of this workshop, I have added this component to the workshop due to an "in the moment situation."

It was a relatively large group in a far too small space which assured mutual collisions. I called a pause and asked one couple to demonstrate the lead for the turn. Then I asked the group what would happen if the follower made the turn. The answer was clear; the follower would run into the next couple. What's a follower to do? It was then that I developed a set of remarks that would be included in every workshop from that moment on.

"When the leader lifts your hand for a turn, it is an invitation, not an order." That explanation alone created an *a-ha!* moment that showed on faces around the room.

"If your leader has asked you to turn 32 times in a row and you don't want to turn, you don't turn. If this invitation would cause you to run into someone else, don't turn. If this invitation would cause a problem for someone not visible to the leader, don't turn. This is an invitation, not an order. You never give up responsibility for your health and safety, or your values and ethics." There were nods across the room, and in a group of students, lots of snapping fingers.

"Of course, it's straightforward to refuse the invitation here in the workshop, and most of the time on a dance floor. Out in the real world though, it becomes a great deal harder. In the real world, a 'no' might mean losing a friend when you stand up to them. It might mean you have to leave the organization. When the organization is your place of work, it can result in the loss of a paycheck and harm to your career. But regardless of the consequences, it's still true. We never abdicate our responsibility for our health and safety – our own and others – or for our values and ethics."

For the leaders, the message is just as clear. One of the first responsibilities of a leader on the dance floor and in an organization is to "do no harm." On the dance floor, this means not initiating a move that will lead your partner to run into someone else or bump up against a table. It means leading in such a way that your partners aren't injured because you tried a trick neither of you was unprepared for. It means paying attention to the movement on the floor and the responses of your partner and choosing your steps and leads accordingly.

In organizations, the concept can be more complicated, but the ideas are the same. You don't ask people to deliver a specialty service to a client when they aren't qualified to do the work. You don't ask staff to use a piece of equipment they haven't been trained to use. You honor them as human beings as best you can within the parameters of the job.

As I said earlier, there are always parts of any job we'd rather not do. Some of them are merely boring and repetitive. Sometimes it means enforcing a policy or practice we disagree with. Along those lines, I am reminded of an introspective question someone once taught me to ask years ago: "Is this a matter of preference or of conscience?" Understanding that difference is critical.

From the leader's perspective, if someone says "no" to our lead from a matter of conscience, it's essential to stop and pay attention. Are they pointing out an aspect of this task or policy we have not yet considered and, if so, what are we going to do with it? If we don't have a problem with the request, but we believe they legitimately do, can their refusal to follow our lead be accommodated? If not, what are our choices? What step will we lead next?

My Professional Ethics professor in law school once told our class: "Only unethical people never face an ethical dilemma." In other words, leading with integrity will mean wrestling with challenging ethical issues every day. Part of a leader's responsibility is to pay attention to the difficult questions and circumstances that arise to have the best chance of leading partners safely and effectively.

Examine your leadership experiences and rate your competence and character in relation to those experiences.

Are there skills you need to develop or hone to improve your competence? If so, what actions can you take to do so?

Have there been times when you had to admit actions were not in line with your integrity, motives, or intent? Take time to identify the reasons for this and the changes you want to make for yourself as you work to become worthy of trust.

Several years ago, I stumbled across Stephen Covey's words (found at the beginning of the chapter) and have taught them in workshops and classes ever since. I have tried to incorporate this concept as a leader *and* as a follower. Followers need leaders who are both competent and confident and who are worthy of their trust. It's the only way the Leadership Dance has any chance of truly being a partnership.

Congruency

I had been working at my new job at a private, church-affiliated college for six months when we began interviewing candidates for a director's job. After finding a promising candidate, I should have been excited. But I wasn't. Why? Because I had had an awkward conversation with my boss that previous day.

While walking with my husband that night, I relayed to him my thoughts. "My supervisor asked about my candidate. Apparently, the president is concerned about hiring a gay man for such a high-profile position because he's getting more pressure about partner benefits," I explained breathlessly. "Adding someone who's in a same-sex relationship could add to that pressure. What happens if I'm told I can't hire him? I won't be able to work there."

After a moment's thought, my husband asked, "Have they asked you to do anything you don't want to do?"

"Well, no."

"Have you finished interviewing all the candidates? Are you ready to send this person an offer?"

"No."

"Then maybe you're borrowing trouble."

And I was…

There was never another conversation like the one I had had with my supervisor. In the end, I did offer my candidate the job because he was the most qualified applicant. And, I'm happy to say, a year later – far sooner than most other colleges and universities – my campus began providing partner benefits to both same-sex and opposite-sex couples with minimum fuss or concern.

I later realized the president had been working on moving his board members toward this outcome and that had been the reason behind the covert conversation my supervisor had had with me.

A critical step in building trust and leading with integrity is to be clear about your values. Understanding what is important to you, the lines you won't cross, and the actions you won't take, make it more likely that your words and actions are congruent.

Lesson 8

Dancing with a New Partner

"It is literally true that you can succeed best and quickest by helping others to succeed."

Napoleon Hill

Change in organizations is always challenging, but fluctuations in leadership can be particularly tricky. It's true even in something as deceptively simple as the Leadership Dance. Participants learn their steps facing a specific person while acting in a particular capacity and then are asked to switch partners and reverse the power dynamics. There is always someone who groans. They've grown comfortable in their role as a follower and now they must switch. Even if the new leader is more confident or a better dancer, they always do something different than the last leader. That means, no matter how capable they are (or aren't), followers have to adjust to match their leaders. Of course, the opposite is also true; leaders must adjust to their followers.

Adjusting to the New

I used to work for a vice president who was a wordsmith and preferred square paperclips. When he retired, we no longer had to keep a box of those special paper clips. While we still worked to maintain a high standard of writing, it was no longer terrifying to submit a written report to the vice president's office since the new person was a mathematician and not critical about word choice. There were other more substantive changes over time, other preferences to learn, but the reality was that we had to change things simply because we had a different leader of our division. In the same way during the workshop when a follower who has become accustomed to a leader giving vocal guidance now has a leader who only uses movement to lead, it can be disconcerting. A shift in leadership means a change in how followers follow.

Sometimes newer leaders don't understand the parallel reality. Leaders need to make their own changes when they move into a new situation. They need to honor organizational history, current culture, and work in progress. New

> When have you experienced change as a follower?
>
> Was it easy or difficult to adjust to a new leader?
>
> What did the new leader do that made the changes simpler or more difficult?

> When have you experienced change as a leader?
>
> What did you do to make the change smoother for the members of your organization?

leaders need to make an effort to understand the skills and talents of their unfamiliar partners and learn what they bring to the partnership. All of that is true, and still, ultimately, it is the responsibility of leaders to set direction, tone, and style. It is also the responsibility of leaders to clearly communicate their expectations, the changes they plan to implement, and engage their followers in the work of making those changes. The ability of leaders to find the balance between honoring the past and current realities while asking their partners to change is often the primary indicator of whether or not the new partnership will be successful.

Support or Sabotage

Often overlooked is the role of the actions of followers in the success or failure of new leaders. Think about a leader entering an existing organization. The opportunities to make a mistake, step on someone's toes, or even, as someone once told me I had done, step "in a sacred cow patty," are nearly endless. Even experienced leaders can quickly find themselves at cross-purposes with their followers.

It can be especially difficult for someone newly appointed to a first leadership position. When leaders are promoted from within, they may know the culture and norms, but there are the additional challenges of dancing a new part with former peers. While leaders are technically in the position of power, they face any number of potential challenges. Similarly, followers are in a position to support a new leader, but can – if they so choose – make life difficult.

Let us revisit the idea of "back leading." If you recall, back leading is when a follower, under the guise of helping the leader find the beat, dance the step correctly, or stay out of trouble, attempts to usurp the role of the leader. This can become a power play, a quarrel between wills that does everything to tear apart the relationship and nothing to advance it. Back leading undermines the ability of leaders to fulfill their responsibilities and causes strife within the dance partnership. On the dance floor, the couple stutters and stumbles along its way. Often, a couple will come to a complete stop, impeding everyone else's ability to enjoy the dance.

> Think of your experiences both with a new leader and as a new leader. As a follower, did you ever exhibit behaviors that were detrimental to the effectiveness of the leader?
>
> As a leader, have you ever experienced a follower who got in your way?
>
> What do these reflections teach you about the role of the follower in the success of a leader?
>
> What do they teach you about the challenges faced by new leaders?

The same can occur in organizations and communities. Members of organizations have unlimited opportunities to sabotage a leader and a surprising number of them are cloaked in support. From the extreme version of a work stoppage or a strike by union members to the subtler but no less damaging loss of necessary paperwork (i.e., refusing to move their feet), followers have a myriad of ways to hinder a leader's progress. In other situations, a follower may sincerely try to aid a leader, but end up getting in the way, confusing matters, or causing unwanted obstacles. Such behavior can result in a tug-of-war over authority and responsibility and, as on the dance floor, result in movement coming to a halt. Even well-meaning followers can be challenging for a new leader who is trying to learn the ways of the organization. Such help can be useful, but can also be a way of resisting change, like saying "This is how we do it here." Leaders need to be able to discern the difference and respond appropriately.

Miscommunication

Early in my career, I hired a new staff member to work in the conduct office. Although this new employee had never done conduct work before, he had been an administrator in a state office which we believed had given him transferable skills.

He was not a good fit unfortunately. His skills and experiences had not prepared him for this type of work. In addition to his lack-luster performance, we were having issues communicating. I thought he wasn't picking up the basics fast enough and he thought I wasn't telling him everything he needed to know to competently do his work. It was true – I had assumed someone with his level of administrative experience would know not to take a non-emergency personal call while meeting with a student about a conduct violation, but that had not been an issue in his prior work. Subsequently, he and I had a number of very difficult conversations.

The school had a six-month probationary period. So, at five months, I told him that I would not be continuing his probationary period. I suggested he start looking for a new job.

Although he wasn't the right person for the job, I admittedly hadn't been an effective leader for him. I had made several false assumptions about his knowledge. From this experience I learned the following:

- It's better to have a vacancy than to hire the wrong person.
- Share your expectations even if you think they are already known to your partners.
- Don't let people push you into making decisions before you are ready. Every partnership has its own learning curve. As the leader, you are the one making the decisions.
- Dancing with a new partner is difficult. There will be miscommunication.
- Every new partner/staff member will provide new opportunities and challenges. Be willing to learn from each one.

Patience Is a Virtue

One of the toughest parts about being a follower on the dance floor is the patience it takes to wait on a novice leader. You can find them in dance studios around the country – the fledgling leader standing still among a sea of swirling couples trying to find the beat. The beginner nods in time with the music or even mutters a count to himself. Then a stutter, a step, and a stop. And through it all, there stands the follower, waiting.

Some followers look long-suffering, tense, and frustrated; some try to help; some try to start and bring the leader along through back leading. None of this is helpful. A select few wait patiently, relaxed, with a pleasant expression on their faces, certain that their leader will eventually get it.

Most of us have leadership and communication styles we prefer in our leaders. We all work at our individual tempos and have different needs for direction and guidance. The reality for followers, on the dance floor and in organizations, is that we have to wait for the leader to set the overall tone and tempo. We take our cues from them.

In our organizations, there is often room for individuality in our daily tasks, but there are times the leader is the one who gets to choose. The *dance* will go much more smoothly if we acknowledge this reality rather than push and pull against the organization's rhythm as set by the leader. We have to learn to follow each leader with his or her different styles and quirks. We have to wait, as patiently as we can, for them to find the rhythm and start the dance.

By developing the patience to learn the leader's cues and rhythm, followers are rewarded by a fundamentally more solid relationship with their new leader. They have learned a new style of dancing or working; they have increased their range and skills. They have learned to be effective followers with a broader range of leaders, which increases their value and popularity both as dancers and as members of the organization.

Likewise, leaders need to exercise patience during a transition. It takes time to understand organizational culture, what programs and processes are working, and which have outlived their usefulness. Even if the new leader's mandate is change, knowing what to change to achieve the desired effect requires time. Leaders who are willing to spend that time getting to know their new partners and organizations have a better chance of navigating the challenges often faced in transitions.

It's also possible for leaders to have too much patience, failing to make a timely decision whether from fear, indecision, or hoping for consensus. At some point, leaders have to act. There are times when everyone can't be involved and the leader has to make a quick decision and then tell people about it later.

Understanding when to be patient and when to act can be one of the most challenging aspects of being a leader. It's also one of those circumstances when a leader has to make the best decision at the time and accept the consequences. Within an organization, it's also one of those times when trustworthiness and history play into the way such actions are received. Followers who trust their leader are more likely to follow a decision without pushback. Leaders who have had the patience to learn about an organization and its people and engage their partners in multiple ways over time are more likely to be supported when they must exercise their authority and decide quickly.

Lesson 9

Be Able to Lead Anyone

"Opportunity dances with those already on the dance floor."

H. Jackson Brown, Jr.

Chapter Three began with the first truth of dancing – it's impossible to dance with people who won't move their feet. The Leadership Dance as a workshop wouldn't work if people weren't willing to suspend their skepticism, move out of their discomfort, and start dancing. Like most of us, I'm best as a leader when I'm working with people who want and are able to accomplish the task I'm leading, complete the changes we need to make, and understand how they are part of a greater purpose. Effective following is an essential component of effective leading.

As I mentioned earlier, dance studios make it easy for people to get on the dance floor with a partner. One method is called the "waterfall." Leaders and followers line up on opposites sides of the floor. Whoever is first in the leader line dances with the first person in the follower line, moving down the floor between the two lines of waiting participants. Then, the second in each line pairs up and so forth. In other words, you dance with whomever is there waiting for you – novice or expert. Since the lines are rarely even, through the course of two or three songs, everyone dances with different partners. The leaders don't get to choose the best dancers or even the best followers. They dance with whomever is standing in front of them.

Dance with the One Who's There

In organizations, followers rarely, if ever, have the opportunity to choose their leaders. While they may be part of an interview process, the final decision rests elsewhere. There are certainly circumstances in which leaders pick their partners. Leaders may get to hire the people who report directly to them. However, for most of us, when we take on a leadership role, we are expected to be able to work with the people already present.

> Think about the different people you have worked with. How do you rate yourself as a leader in your ability to work with a wide variety of partners?

The Leadership Dance design isn't technically a "waterfall," but the principles are the same – mix people up and give everyone a chance to dance with different partners. At a dance studio, some couples come to the studio for the single purpose of wanting to learn to dance together; they prefer not to rotate partners in class or to participate in the waterfall. Instructors generally respect that preference, though they encourage rotation. They do so because they know dancing with different partners is an opportunity to learn more skills in leading and following.

The same is true in organizations. Each time we work with someone new, we have a chance to learn from them – if we are open to the experience. Working with different people pushes us to test new methods of doing our work, to apply different skills, and to find new ways of accomplishing goals. This reality is true for every member of an organization.

Leaders need to be able to work with partners whose skills and knowledge vary widely. They need to be able to work with partners who may not be confident about their ability to do the necessary work. Because leaders will work with people who prefer to receive information in a variety of ways, they need to be able to communicate using diverse communication styles. This reality is one of the reasons leadership is so challenging. Leaders don't get to learn one set of behaviors that work well and then keep repeating them over and over. Effective leaders adapt and learn to dance with and lead partners who are standing before them whatever their skill level.

> Think about leaders you have known. Identify those who were particularly adept at working with a variety of people.
>
> What can you learn from them?

Carry Your Own Weight

Years ago, I competed in several national dance competitions. For one in particular, I went all out and danced about 100 heats over the two and a half days of competition. My partner was my dance teacher and he was dancing with two or three other students as well. In other words, he was dancing a lot!

Mid-morning on the second day, he gathered us together and made this pronouncement, "Y'all have got to start carrying your own weight. You have to hold your own arms up. You can't keep resting them on mine!"

Think about it. Hours upon hours holding his right arm up in the air with partners comfortably resting their left arms on his. He was used to being on his feet for long stretches of time, but we were pushing him past his ability to carry his weight and ours. Leaders need partners who are responsible for their own success, who can carry their own weight.

Weight is a surprisingly important part of the dance equation. This doesn't mean how much you weigh, mind you, but how you carry your weight.

Each of us has a center of gravity which *Physiopedia* describes as "a point from which the weight of a body or system may be considered to act… [It] lies approximately anterior to the second sacral vertebra. However, since human beings do not remain fixed in the anatomical position, the precise location of the center of gravity changes constantly with every new position of the body and limbs."

Physiopedia Contributors. 7 October 2019. *Physiopedia*. Accessed December 9, 2019. https://www.physio-pedia.com/index.php?title=Centre_of_Gravity&oldid=224098)

While you might not think so at first, these are helpful definitions for dancers. As individuals, we move from our own center of gravity. Because an individual's center of gravity can shift as they change positions, it becomes an essential element when dancing with a partner. In a partnership, we have to move together to create a shared center of gravity from which we can act.

Followers who aren't strong enough to carry their own weight, who rely on the leader to move them, or who need to be pulled along, aren't any fun to dance with; they are difficult, if not impossible to lead on the dance floor and in organizations. Even when you don't have the leadership responsibility, it's challenging to work with someone who doesn't meet their obligations, who can't handle their part of the job. While the leader has the role of initiating the dance and the work, our organizations and communities need everyone to be responsible for their own tasks and to step up and share responsibility for the success of any venture.

Have you ever worked with someone who wasn't able or willing to carry his or her own weight? Think about what it looked and felt like.

Now, ask yourself – are you carrying your own weight?

If you have the leadership role, what would you need to do to help others understand how to shoulder their responsibilities?

Grace and Forgiveness

Grace and forgiveness aren't words we typically hear in discussions about leadership perhaps because they feel religiously-charged. Whether or not that's the reason, we need more of each in both our organizations and our leadership partnerships. Leadership is an ever-shifting, dynamic role; it's all about people who have a range of skills, talents, personalities, and quirks. When coupled with the pressure that arises from trying to accomplish a task together, the results can be stressful. Even the most talented, well-meaning partners make mistakes from time to time.

I continue to be surprised by how little kindness and courtesy seem to be valued in leadership. Maybe it goes back to the idea of needing to be a strong leader or understanding leadership as directing activity rather than partnering with others to achieve a goal. Whatever the reason, a bit of courtesy on the part of both leaders and followers goes a long way toward developing a successful partnership.

Being considerate of others doesn't equate to being weak or ineffectual. For leaders, it should involve owning your mistakes and taking responsibility for your own need to learn a new skill among other things. From a follower's perspective, it might also mean acknowledging that leaders are human too and granting them the opportunity to learn and improve in their capabilities.

Now, let's be clear. I'm not talking about malfeasance, harassment, the failure to do a job, or any of the other ways people can actively engage in bad behavior. On the dance floor, you have every right to stop dancing with someone who doesn't respect your boundaries or is actually hurting you. In organizations, we have a responsibility to stop any behavior that is harming people, morale, or the work of the organization.

Partners who practice grace and forgiveness on the dance floor find they are valued as partners no matter their skill level. No matter which role they play, their partners aren't worried or defensive about making mistakes. As a result, they relax, make fewer mistakes, and have more fun.

In organizations, leaders who show grace and practice forgiveness, who understand failure as a necessary step to growth and learning, will often find they are working with partners who are creative, willing to take on new challenges, and glad to shoulder the work of the organization.

Followers who show grace and forgiveness may be more likely to find leaders and peers who want to support them in their work and their personal development. Grace and forgiveness are essential to a successful partnership, no matter the type or the purpose.

Rate yourself on your ability to work with a wide variety of partners. Are there people you struggle to work alongside? If so, what do you need to do to expand your skill set?

Do you carry your own weight? How do you help people learn to be responsible for their own success within an organization?

Finally, think about the ideas of grace and forgiveness. Are there times you now wish you had been able to extend grace and forgive a misstep? Are there current situations that might call for either of these attributes? How might you bring them into your leadership practice?

Conclusion

"Beginning dancer: knows nothing.
Intermediate dancer: knows everything; is too good to dance with beginners.
Hotshot dancer: too good to dance with anyone.
Advanced dancer: dances everything, especially with beginners."

Richard Crum

Everyone starts off as a beginner, a novice, a newcomer. Whether you're a dancer or a leader, a follower or an instructor, everyone starts off as an apprentice of some sort. The most skilled, fluid dancer was once an awkward learner nodding to keep time with the music. It is through experience, trial and error, and shared understanding that we as a collective move forward.

I began my dance lessons bumbling into my partner and miscalculating the distance between our feet. But as I gained competency, my confidence blossomed. Through dance, I learned basic leadership skills – not enough to lead in a major competition, mind you, but enough to reach out to newcomers and give them guidance.

As I grew in dance floor aptitude, I attracted a full range of dancers because, although I could lead, I could also follow. I could read the nuances of a subtle lead while minimizing the effects of a leader's mistakes; similarly, I could alter my lead to accommodate a novice's uncertain steps. With experience, I became an all-around good partner.

Upon discovering that the world of ballroom dance was most popular with women, which traditionally meant the ratio of leaders to followers was uneven, I began joining in beginners' classes to learn to lead. While I was not an expert by any stretch of the imagination, I was a leader who remembered what it was like to be a follower. I knew the patterns and the mistakes most common to beginners. I was certain I could help them succeed.

Once on the dance floor though, I realized how challenging it was to be a good leader. Knowing the patterns was crucial to the formation of the dance, but leading required other skills. As a new leader, I had to plan the next steps, predict the flow of the music, observe and maneuver around other couples, and give my own partner accurate and precise cues that properly communicated my intentions. It was then that I realized being a follower was just as important as being a leader. My appreciation for the unsung followers in my life grew. There can be no leaders without followers; followers matter.

It was the indomitable Bruce Lee who said, "When one has reached maturity in the art, one will have a formless form. It is like ice dissolving in water. When one has no form, one can be all forms; when one has no style, one can fit in with any style." It is only through mutual understanding that leaders and followers are able to realize how imperative the other's role is.

Leadership and management should not be one person driving a team of subordinates like a dog sled team running the Iditarod. Leadership is a partnership, a dance. It is working together in pursuit of a shared purpose and collective goal. Leaders are not inherently better than followers nor more important, because without followers, there would be no leaders. Similarly, if within a group there are no leaders, then the group remains stagnant. Without a leader who knows the patterns, who knows the music, who knows the steps, the group remains ineffectual.

Both leaders and followers must know what to expect of each other. Leaders must clearly and concisely convey direction and know-how while followers provide the energy and momentum to drive the group forward.

Only when both leaders and followers move in the same direction, whether it is across a dance floor or toward a critical organization goal, is the dynamic power of leadership as partnership unleashed.

Acknowledgements

This book wouldn't have been possible without the, literally, hundreds of good-natured people who have participated in The Leadership Dance workshops over the past 15 years. Each group and every individual taught me lessons about leadership, dance, and facilitation. All of that learning has gone into the writing of this book.

Equal credit goes to the many people I have worked with throughout my career. Their support and patience as I have practiced leadership have made all the difference. Any reputation I have as a leader is due to the fact that I have worked with extraordinary people.

Writing a book is a complex process and there are many people who have supported me along the way. Unfortunately, I can't name them all, but special recognition needs to go to the colleagues and friends who have been readers, editors, and cheerleaders – Edna Dominguez, Sharon Justice, Cathryn Cole, and Becky Spurlock.

To Kara Scrivener of Emerging Ink Solutions for providing great editing, giving me deadlines and assignments, and helping me shape a mass of words into a book – thank you. To Amanda Eyre Ward's writing seminar which introduced me to people who actually write books and helped me learn to write a book rather than be someone who thinks about writing a book – thank you.

And in the sense of movie credits where the really important actor's name comes at the very end, my thanks to my husband, Peter Geenberg. Not only does he review and edit my work-a-day writing of proposals, blogs, and newsletters, he has always supported me every time I get a new idea – no matter how crazy.

About the Author

Gage E. Paine is the founder of Gage Paine Consulting, a consulting firm designed to support higher education and non-profit leaders who want to make a difference in their organizations and communities. She brings to this work more than 30 years of experience in higher education, including service as a vice president for three universities – Trinity University, The University of Texas at San Antonio, and The University of Texas at Austin.

Known for her creativity, her use of dance, yoga, and poetry in workshops and speeches, and recognized nationally as a leader in higher education, she is sought after as a facilitator, leadership coach, and speaker. Her resumé lists more than 100 speeches, presentations, and panels including her talk at TEDxSanAntonio in 2012. She has taught undergraduate courses in leadership at both SMU and Trinity University in San Antonio.

Outside of her work, Gage loves to read, knit, and, of course, dance. She lives in San Marcos, Texas with her husband of 30 years and two dogs. If she ever wins the lottery, she's going full-in on ballroom dancing to buy all of the glittery dresses and ball gowns.

Made in the USA
Monee, IL
08 June 2021